The Best of Times

Math Strategies That Multiply

★ ★ ★

BY Greg Tang

ILLUSTRATED BY
Harry Briggs

SCHOLASTIC PRESS • NEW YORK

Author's Note

Do you remember learning to spell? Remember how much easier it was once you could sound out words and letters? With a basic understanding and a few rules, all of a sudden spelling wasn't so hard! Now think back to when you learned to multiply. If you were like most people, you probably memorized your times tables. There was very little understanding or real math involved, just a lot of repetition and maybe a trick or two like using your knuckles to learn the nines table. But is that the best way to learn?

Instead, wouldn't it be great if by understanding math better you could learn to multiply numbers of any size, not just the ones you memorize? I believe it's possible. By being clever and using a little common sense, kids can learn to multiply large and small numbers quickly and dependably. Multiply by four? Just double twice. Multiply by five? First multiply by ten, then take half. These strategies are simple and easy to remember because they make sense. There's no fancy math involved, just straightforward techniques that really work.

I wrote *The Best of Times* to help kids master their times tables. But instead of taking a short-term approach based on repetition and memorization, my focus is on the longer-term and helping children develop a sounder, more intuitive understanding of multiplication. I use poems and pictures to convey and clarify concepts, and throughout the book, I challenge readers to apply what they've learned so they see firsthand how fun and rewarding problem-solving can be. In writing *The Grapes of Math, Math for All Seasons,* and now *The Best of Times*, my goal is to inspire kids to seek a deeper, more satisfying understanding of math. It is this journey of learning that truly is the best of times. Enjoy!

Greg Tang

With love to Gregory —
you have taught me so much
— G.T.

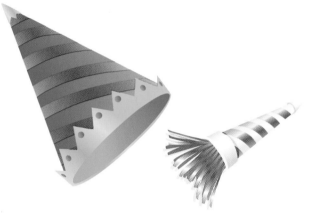

To my mother,
Ingrid Ekelin
— H.B.

Absolute Zero

Zero is a cinch to do,
   the answer's right in front of you.
For every problem it's the same,
   zilch or zero is its name!

$0 \times 0 =$

$0 \times 5 =$

$0 \times 32 =$

$0 \times 273 =$

$0 \times 459 =$

Find the answers at the end of the book!

One Way

One is simple as can be,
it's known as the identity.
The answer to identify?
It's the one you multiply!

Challenge: What is 1 x 31? 1 x 365?

Two Step

Two is very fast and fun,
    quickly double and you're done.
What's that you say, be more precise?
    Okay then, just add it twice!

What is 2 x 2? It's 2 doubled.

$$2 + 2 = 4$$

What is 2 x 8? It's 8 doubled.

$$2 \times 8 = 8 + 8$$
$$= 16$$

Challenge: What is 2 x 12? 2 x 44?

Three Sum

Three is as easy as can be,
  if you triple what you see.
In other words just add it thrice,
  this simply is one more than twice!

What is 3 x 3?   It's 3 doubled plus 3.

Double first: Then add 3:

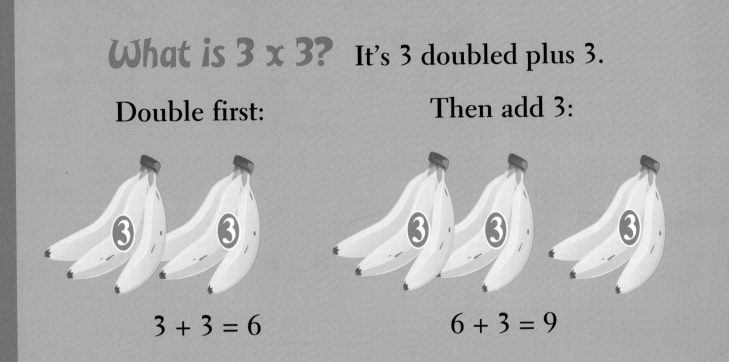

3 + 3 = 6   6 + 3 = 9

What is 3 x 9?   It's 9 doubled plus 9.

$$3 \times 9 = (9 + 9) + 9$$
$$= \quad 18 \quad + 9$$
$$= \quad 27$$

Challenge: What is 3 x 15? 3 x 33?

Four Eyes

Four is very fast to do,
when you multiply by 2.
Here's a little good advice –
please just always double twice!

What is 4 x 4? It's 4 doubled twice.

Double once: Double twice:

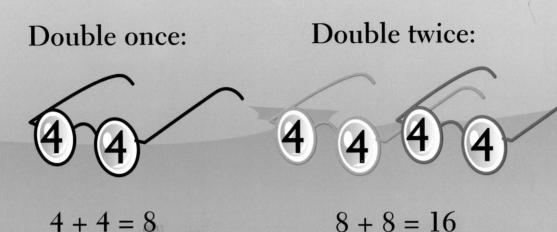

4 + 4 = 8   8 + 8 = 16

What is 4 x 7? It's 7 doubled twice.

Double once: 7 + 7 = 14
Double twice: 14 + 14 = 28

Challenge: What is 4 x 14? 4 x 35?

Five Alive

Five will yield the right amount,
    if by 5's you always count.
Or else just multiply by 10,
    half will get you there again!

What is 5 x 5? It's ten 5's divided in half.

$$50 \div 2 = 25$$

What is 5 x 8? It's ten 8's divided in half.

$$5 \times 8 = (10 \times 8) \div 2$$
$$= \quad 80 \quad \div 2$$
$$= \quad 40$$

Challenge: What is 5 x 16? 5 x 48?

Six Sense

Six is pretty quick to do,
    just multiply by 3 then 2.
If this sounds like too much trouble,
    triple first before you double!

What is 6 x 6? It's 6 tripled, then doubled.

Triple first:

Then double:

$6 + 6 + 6 = 18$

$18 + 18 = 36$

What is 6 x 4? It's 4 tripled, then doubled.

Triple first: $4 + 4 + 4 = 12$

Then double: $12 + 12 = 24$

Challenge: What is 6 x 15? 6 x 33?

Seven Heaven

Seven doesn't take much time,
even though it is a prime.
Here is all you have to do,
first times 5 then add times 2!

What is 7 x 7? It's five 7's plus two 7's.

$$35 + 14 = 49$$

What is 7 x 5? It's five 5's plus two 5's.

$$7 \times 5 = (5 \times 5) + (2 \times 5)$$
$$= \quad 25 \quad + \quad 10$$
$$= \quad 35$$

Challenge: What is 7 x 14? 7 x 22?

Crazy Eight

Eight is very much like four,
    simply double but once more.
Since 2 times 2 times 2 is 8,
    doubling three times works just great!

What is 8 x 8? It's 8 doubled three times.

Double once: Double twice: Double three times:

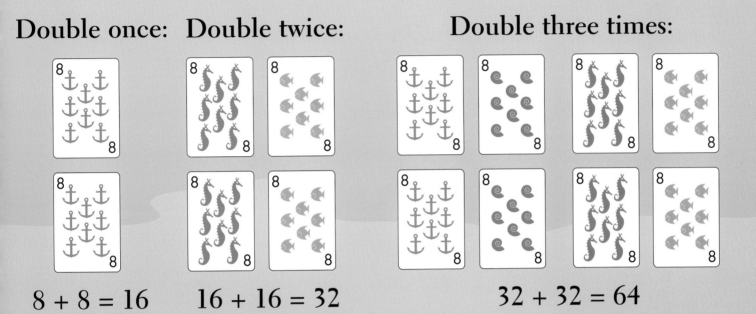

8 + 8 = 16   16 + 16 = 32   32 + 32 = 64

What is 8 x 6? It's 6 doubled three times.

Double once: 6 + 6 = 12
Double twice: 12 + 12 = 24
Double three times: 24 + 24 = 48

Challenge: What is 8 x 25? What is 8 x 35?

Nine Ball

Nine is faster to compute,
 if at first you overshoot.
Here's a very clever tack,
 do 10 times and then subtract!

What is 9 x 9? It's ten 9's minus 9.

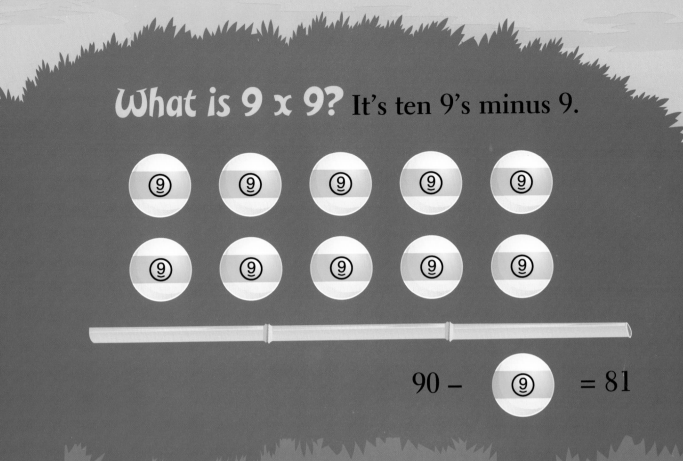

$$90 - 9 = 81$$

What is 9 x 7? It's ten 7's minus 7.

$$9 \times 7 = (10 \times 7) - 7$$
$$= 70 - 7$$
$$= 63$$

Challenge: What is 9 x 12? What is 9 x 34?

Perfect Ten

Ten is such a breeze to do,
    all because of place value.
To quickly multiply by 10,
    put a zero at the end!

What is 10 x 10? It's 10 with a zero on the end.

What is 10 x 9? It's 9 with a zero on the end.

$$10 \times 9 = 90$$

Challenge: What is 10 x 18? 10 x 72?

Practice Tables

Absolute Zero

"For every problem it's the same, zilch or zero is its name!"

0 x	1	=	0
0 x	2	=	0
0 x	3	=	0
0 x	4	=	0
0 x	5	=	0
0 x	6	=	0
0 x	7	=	0
0 x	8	=	0
0 x	9	=	0
0 x	10	=	0
0 x	24	=	0
0 x	99	=	0

One Way

"The answer to identify? It's the one you multiply!"

1 x	1	=	1
1 x	2	=	2
1 x	3	=	3
1 x	4	=	4
1 x	5	=	5
1 x	6	=	6
1 x	7	=	7
1 x	8	=	8
1 x	9	=	9
1 x	10	=	10
1 x	31	=	31
1 x	365	=	365

Two Step

	Double
2 x 1	1 + 1 = 2
2 x 2	2 + 2 = 4
2 x 3	3 + 3 = 6
2 x 4	4 + 4 = 8
2 x 5	5 + 5 = 10
2 x 6	6 + 6 = 12
2 x 7	7 + 7 = 14
2 x 8	8 + 8 = 16
2 x 9	9 + 9 = 18
2 x 10	10 + 10 = 20
2 x 12	12 + 12 = 24
2 x 44	44 + 44 = 88

"Two is very fast and fun, quickly double and you're done!"

Three Sum

	Double	Add One More
3 x 1	1 + 1 = 2	2 + 1 = 3
3 x 2	2 + 2 = 4	4 + 2 = 6
3 x 3	3 + 3 = 6	6 + 3 = 9
3 x 4	4 + 4 = 8	8 + 4 = 12
3 x 5	5 + 5 = 10	10 + 5 = 15
3 x 6	6 + 6 = 12	12 + 6 = 18
3 x 7	7 + 7 = 14	14 + 7 = 21
3 x 8	8 + 8 = 16	16 + 8 = 24
3 x 9	9 + 9 = 18	18 + 9 = 27
3 x 10	10 + 10 = 20	20 + 10 = 30
3 x 15	15 + 15 = 30	30 + 15 = 45
3 x 33	33 + 33 = 66	66 + 33 = 99

"For three you simply add it thrice, in other words one more than twice!"

Four Eyes

"Here's a little good advice— please just always double twice!"

	Double Once	Double Twice
4 x 1	1 + 1 = 2	2 + 2 = 4
4 x 2	2 + 2 = 4	4 + 4 = 8
4 x 3	3 + 3 = 6	6 + 6 = 12
4 x 4	4 + 4 = 8	8 + 8 = 16
4 x 5	5 + 5 = 10	10 + 10 = 20
4 x 6	6 + 6 = 12	12 + 12 = 24
4 x 7	7 + 7 = 14	14 + 14 = 28
4 x 8	8 + 8 = 16	16 + 16 = 32
4 x 9	9 + 9 = 18	18 + 18 = 36
4 x 10	10 + 10 = 20	20 + 20 = 40
4 x 14	14 + 14 = 28	28 + 28 = 56
4 x 35	35 + 35 = 70	70 + 70 = 140

Five Alive

"First just multiply by 10, half will get you there again!"

	Times 10	Divide by 2
5 x 1	1 x 10 = 10	10 ÷ 2 = 5
5 x 2	2 x 10 = 20	20 ÷ 2 = 10
5 x 3	3 x 10 = 30	30 ÷ 2 = 15
5 x 4	4 x 10 = 40	40 ÷ 2 = 20
5 x 5	5 x 10 = 50	50 ÷ 2 = 25
5 x 6	6 x 10 = 60	60 ÷ 2 = 30
5 x 7	7 x 10 = 70	70 ÷ 2 = 35
5 x 8	8 x 10 = 80	80 ÷ 2 = 40
5 x 9	9 x 10 = 90	90 ÷ 2 = 45
5 x 10	10 x 10 = 100	100 ÷ 2 = 50
5 x 16	16 x 10 = 160	160 ÷ 2 = 80
5 x 48	48 x 10 = 480	480 ÷ 2 = 240

	Triple First	Then Double
6 x 1	1 + 1 + 1 = 3	3 + 3 = 6
6 x 2	2 + 2 + 2 = 6	6 + 6 = 12
6 x 3	3 + 3 + 3 = 9	9 + 9 = 18
6 x 4	4 + 4 + 4 = 12	12 + 12 = 24
6 x 5	5 + 5 + 5 = 15	15 + 15 = 30
6 x 6	6 + 6 + 6 = 18	18 + 18 = 36
6 x 7	7 + 7 + 7 = 21	21 + 21 = 42
6 x 8	8 + 8 + 8 = 24	24 + 24 = 48
6 x 9	9 + 9 + 9 = 27	27 + 27 = 54
6 x 10	10 + 10 + 10 = 30	30 + 30 = 60
6 x 15	15 + 15 + 15 = 45	45 + 45 = 90
6 x 33	33 + 33 + 33 = 99	99 + 99 = 198

Six Sense

"Six is pretty quick to do, just multiply by 3 then 2!"

	First Times 5	Add Times 2
7 x 1	(1 x 10) ÷ 2 = 5	5 + 2 = 7
7 x 2	(2 x 10) ÷ 2 = 10	10 + 4 = 14
7 x 3	(3 x 10) ÷ 2 = 15	15 + 6 = 21
7 x 4	(4 x 10) ÷ 2 = 20	20 + 8 = 28
7 x 5	(5 x 10) ÷ 2 = 25	25 + 10 = 35
7 x 6	(6 x 10) ÷ 2 = 30	30 + 12 = 42
7 x 7	(7 x 10) ÷ 2 = 35	35 + 14 = 49
7 x 8	(8 x 10) ÷ 2 = 40	40 + 16 = 56
7 x 9	(9 x 10) ÷ 2 = 45	45 + 18 = 63
7 x 10	(10 x 10) ÷ 2 = 50	50 + 20 = 70
7 x 14	(14 x 10) ÷ 2 = 70	70 + 28 = 98
7 x 22	(22 x 10) ÷ 2 = 110	110 + 44 = 154

Seven Heaven

"Seven is a circh to do, first times 5 then add times 2!"

Crazy Eight

"Since 2 times 2 times 2 is 8, doubling 3 times works just great!"

	Double Once	Double Twice	Double 3x
8 x 1	1 + 1 = 2	2 + 2 = 4	4 + 4 = 8
8 x 2	2 + 2 = 4	4 + 4 = 8	8 + 8 = 16
8 x 3	3 + 3 = 6	6 + 6 = 12	12 + 12 = 24
8 x 4	4 + 4 = 8	8 + 8 = 16	16 + 16 = 32
8 x 5	5 + 5 = 10	10 + 10 = 20	20 + 20 = 40
8 x 6	6 + 6 = 12	12 + 12 = 24	24 + 24 = 48
8 x 7	7 + 7 = 14	14 + 14 = 28	28 + 28 = 56
8 x 8	8 + 8 = 16	16 + 16 = 32	32 + 32 = 64
8 x 9	9 + 9 = 18	18 + 18 = 36	36 + 36 = 72
8 x 10	10 + 10 = 20	20 + 20 = 40	40 + 40 = 80
8 x 25	25 + 25 = 50	50 + 50 = 100	100 + 100 = 200
8 x 35	35 + 35 = 70	70 + 70 = 140	140 + 140 = 280

Nine Ball

"Here's a very clever tack, do 10 times and then subtract!"

	Do 10x	Subtract 1x
9 x 1	10 x 1 = 10	10 – 1 = 9
9 x 2	10 x 2 = 20	20 – 2 = 18
9 x 3	10 x 3 = 30	30 – 3 = 27
9 x 4	10 x 4 = 40	40 – 4 = 36
9 x 5	10 x 5 = 50	50 – 5 = 45
9 x 6	10 x 6 = 60	60 – 6 = 54
9 x 7	10 x 7 = 70	70 – 7 = 63
9 x 8	10 x 8 = 80	80 – 8 = 72
9 x 9	10 x 9 = 90	90 – 9 = 81
9 x 10	10 x 10 = 100	100 – 10 = 90
9 x 12	10 x 12 = 120	120 – 12 = 108
9 x 34	10 x 34 = 340	340 – 34 = 306

Put a Zero at the End

10 x	1	=	10
10 x	2	=	20
10 x	3	=	30
10 x	4	=	40
10 x	5	=	50
10 x	6	=	60
10 x	7	=	70
10 x	8	=	80
10 x	9	=	90
10 x	10	=	100
10 x	18	=	180
10 x	72	=	720

Perfect Ten

"To quickly multiply by 10, put a zero at the end!"

Special thanks to Liz Szabla for her faith in me;
to Kate Egan for her patience, perseverance, and good
judgment; and to Jean Feiwel for making it all happen.

LIBRARY OF CONGRESS CATALOGING-IN-PUBLICATION DATA
Tang, Greg. Best of times / by Greg Tang ; illustrated by Harry Briggs.—1st ed.
p. cm.   Summary: Simple rhymes offer hints on how to multiply any number
by zero through ten without memorizing the multiplication tables.
1. Multiplication—Juvenile literature. [1. Multiplication.] I. Briggs, Harry. ill. II. Title.
QA115.T357 2002 513.2'13—dc21 2002023043
ISBN 0-439-21044-5
10 9 8 7 6 5 4 3 2 1   02 03 04 05 06
Printed in Mexico 49 • First edition, September 2002

The text type was set in Electra Regular. The display type was set in WacWacOoops!
Harry Briggs's artwork was created on computer. Book design by David Caplan